workbook

To my parents the brightest guiding lights

Copyright © 2017 Laura Paulisich
Photographs copyright © 2017 Laura Paulisich
www.laurapaulisich.com

All rights reserved.
First Printing, 2017
ISBN 978-0-998-18998-7

Design by Laura Paulisich

REASONS

HAPPINESS:
"Happiness does not just make you enjoy life more; it actually affects how successful you are in both your personal life and your professional life."-Richard Wiseman

WRITING:
"Each [writing] entry taking just a few moments...According to scientific studies, you should quickly notice the difference in mood and happiness, changes that may persist for months. If you feel the effects wearing off, simply repeat the exercise." -Richard Wiseman

"[writing may] decrease anxiety and depression related intrusive thoughts [according to] two dozen studies using a number of populations around the world" -Mar & Peterson

"people who wrote about their best possible selves scored higher on measures of psychological well-being (including happiness and life satisfaction)"-Richard Wiseman

"people who wrote about ideal lives visisted medical professionals less" -Richard Wiseman

GRATITUDE LISTING:
"subjects who reflected on the good things in their life once a week by writing them down were more positive and motivated about their current situations and their futures" -Richard Wiseman

VALUES & GOALS:
"One path to happiness clearly appears to lie in the identification and pursuit of personally relevant goals... In the words of the authors: 'This finding suggests that those people who can identify sets of goals that well represent their implicit interests and values are indeed able to function more efficiently, flexibly, and integratively across all areas of their lives' (emphasis added)."

TRACKING *(checklists)* **& ACCOUNTABILITY FOR CHANGING HABITS:**
"Research has repeatedly found that when behavior is tracked and evaluated, it improves drastically... When you track something, you become aware of it. When you report something, you become accountable to it." - Benjamin P. Hardy-

READING:
"Ordinary people seek entertainment. Extraordinary people seek education and learning. It is common for the world's most successful people to read at least one book per week. They are constantly learning." -Benjamin P. Hardy

TAKING RISKS & ASKING:
"courageously confront fear for 20 seconds every single day, before you know it, you'll be in a different socioeconomic and social situation...make that call, ask that question, pitch that idea, post that video, whatever it is you feel you want to do - do it" -Benjamin P. Hardy

EARLY SLEEPING/RISING:
"Harvard biologist Christopher Randler found that early sleep/risers are more proactive and more likely to anticipate problems and minimize them efficiently which leads to being more successful in business, better planner, being holistically healthier, better sleep, more optimistic, satisfied, conscientious"

PURPOSE & FULFILLMENT:
What matters most? 24 hours... week... month... 6 months...

January

"Picture a place where there is nothing to fear and all of your dreams have come true!" -Martha Beck

If you could do ANYTHING without worrying about family, friends, societal pressures, time, money, education, etc., what would you do?! Write, draw, list anything that comes to mind describing your perfect day/week/month/life!

Monthly Inventory

books read:

1
2
3
4
5

new learning/new experience/new connection:

risks taken:

accomplishments or favorite happenings:

contributions to the world:

DAILY CHECKLIST

	M	T	W	Th	F	Sa	Su
Did I sleep in total darkness?							
Did I sleep in total darkness? Did I stop looking at monitors 2 hours before sleeping?							
Did I sleep in total darkness? *Did I stop looking at monitors 2 hours before sleeping?* Did I stay in bed and keep my eyes closed if unable to sleep?							
Did I sleep in total darkness? *Did I stop looking at monitors 2 hours before sleeping?* *Did I stay in bed and keep my eyes closed if unable to sleep?* Did I wake naturally without an alarm? (went to bed at a time that allowed me to wake naturally)							

#SHINE

February

"How we spend our time is, of course, how we spend our lives." -Annie Dillard

List the activitis of a typical day and record if the activity caused stress and why.

Activity, duration times: *Stress or contentment (why?):*

Febr

Monthly Inventory

books read:

1
2
3
4
5

new learning/new experience/new connection:

risks taken:

accomplishments or favorite happenings:

contributions to the world:

DAILY CHECKLIST

	M	T	W	Th	F	Sa	Su
Did I find the purest ingredients made from nature and cook the ingredients slowly at low temperatures?							
Did I find the purest ingredients made from nature and cook the ingredients slowly at low temperatures? Did I walk and/or exercise at least 40 minutes before eating in the morning?							
Did I find the purest ingredients made from nature and cook the ingredients slowly at low temperatures? *Did I walk and/or exercise at least 40 minutes before eating in the morning?* Did I chew all food completely?							
Did I find the purest ingredients made from nature and cook the ingredients slowly at low temperatures? *Did I walk and/or exercise at least 40 minutes before eating in the morning?* *Did I chew all food completely?* Did I drink filtered, remineralized water 15 minutes before eating and 2 hours after eating?							

#SHINE

abundance acceptance accountability achievement **advancement** adventure advocacy ambition appreciation attractiveness boldness brilliance beauty calmness caring challenge charity cheerfulness clarity cleverness **contemplative** community compassion cooperation collaboration contribution creativity curiosity daring decisiveness dedication dependability diversity dynamic empathy encouragement **enthusiasm** ethics excellence expressiveness fairness family friendships flexibility freedom fun **generosity** grace growth flexibility health happiness harmonious honesty honor humility humor independence individuality innovation inspiration intelligence intuition **joy** kindness knowledge leadership learning loyalty loving making-a-difference mindfulness **meditative** motivation nature optimism open-minded originality passion performance peaceful persistent playful powerful popular prideful professional purpose quality relationships reliability resilience resourcefulness respectful **responsible** security selflessness self-love simplicity spiritual spontaneous stability status strong success teamwork thankfulness thoughtfulness traditionalism trustworthy understanding unique **useful** versatile vision warmth wealth wisdom

Think like a PROTON. Always POSITIVE. :)

March

"**What value does your life demonstrate the most?** What do you presently fill your personal space with the most and what do you presently spend the most time, energy, money, thought, vision, internal and external conversation on, what inspires you, what are your goals and what do you love to learn?" -Preston Palmer

List 3 words that most accurately describe each topic.

personal space:

time:

energy:

money:

thought:

vision:

conversation:

inspiration:

goals:

love to learn:

Top three repeated words and how many times each word was repeated:

Based on your current top 3 values, write 3 goals for the next 3 months.

1._____

Why is this goal important?
What ACTION will you add to achieve this goal?
When?

2._____

Why is this goal important?
What ACTION will you add to achieve this goal?
When?

3._____

Why is this goal important?
What ACTION will you add to achieve this goal?
When?

Add ACTIONS to calendar dates!

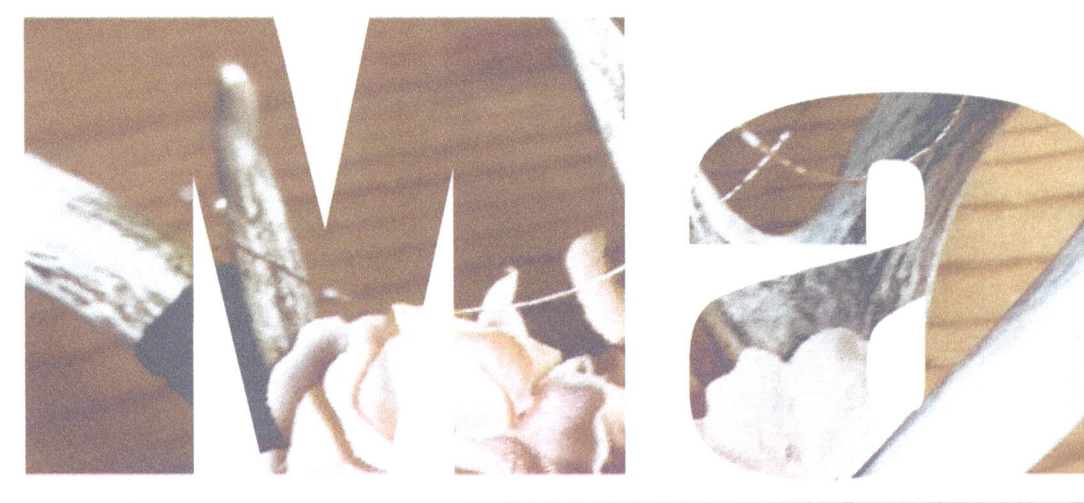

Monthly Inventory

books read:

1
2
3
4
5

new learning/new experience/new connection:

risks taken:

accomplishments or favorite happenings:

contributions to the world:

DAILY CHECKLIST

	M	T	W	Th	F	Sa	Su
Did I move/exercise/walk (2 hours walking = natural)?							
Did I move/exercise/walk (2 hours walking = natural)? Did I stand straight, posture up, chin up?							
Did I move/exercise/walk (2 hours walking = natural)? *Did I stand straight, posture up, chin up?* Did I stand rather than sit?							
Did I move/exercise/walk (2 hours walking = natural)? *Did I stand straight, posture up, chin up?* *Did I stand rather than sit?* Did I take stairs (not elevator) and/or walk (not drive) whenever possible?							

April

"Those who spent just a few minutes engaged in affectionate writing showing a marked increase in happiness, a reduction in stress, and even a significant decrease in their cholesterol levels...

Think about someone who is very important to you. Imagine that you only have one opportunity to tell this person how important they are to you. Write a short letter to this person, describing how much you care for them and the impact that they have had on your life." -Richard Wiseman

Monthly Inventory

books read:

1
2
3
4
5

new learning/new experience/new connection:

risks taken:

accomplishments or favorite happenings:

contributions to the world:

DAILY CHECKLIST

	M	T	W	Th	F	Sa	Su
Did I go outside at least 30 minutes?							
Did I go outside at least 30 minutes?							
Did I go outside at least 30 minutes?							
Did I go outside at least 30 minutes?							

#SHINE

May

What are the things you absolutely MUST do before you die? Imagine having 30 days to live. Imagine having 5 years to live.

Monthly Inventory

books read:

1
2
3
4
5

new learning/new experience/new connection:

risks taken:

accomplishments or favorite happenings:

contributions to the world:

DAILY CHECKLIST

	M	T	W	Th	F	Sa	Su
Did I laugh and/or make myself laugh?							
Did I laugh and/or make myself laugh? Did I smile and/or hold a smile?							
Did I laugh and/or make myself laugh? *Did I smile and/or hold a smile?* Did I offer a smile to a stranger?							
Did I laugh and/or make myself laugh? *Did I smile and/or hold a smile?* *Did I offer a smile to a stranger?* Did I offer a compliment to a stranger?							

#SHINE

June

Notes to remember about past three goals:

What did I do well?

How can I improve and keep going?

Write 3 more goals for the next 3 months.

1._____

Why is this goal important?
What ACTION will you add to achieve this goal?
When?

2._____

Why is this goal important?
What ACTION will you add to achieve this goal?
When?

3._____

Why is this goal important?
What ACTION will you add to achieve this goal?
When?

Add ACTIONS to calendar dates!

Monthly Inventory

books read:

1
2
3
4
5

new learning/new experience/new connection:

risks taken:

accomplishments or favorite happenings:

contributions to the world:

DAILY CHECKLIST

	M	T	W	Th	F	Sa	Su
Did I walk relaxed?							
Did I walk relaxed? Did I swing my arms?							
Did I walk relaxed? *Did I swing my arms?* Did I put a spring in my step?							
Did I walk relaxed? *Did I swing my arms?* *Did I put a spring in my step?* Did I nod my head and use expressive gestures?							

#SHINE

July

What do iLOVE about myself?

What are things I like and dislike about my actions?

How do I express LOVE for myself?

Besides people, what else do iLOVE?

What are five ways I have acted lovingly toward others?

How have I been unkind toward someone who is important to me?

What can I do today that will show my love for others and for myself?

-Blueprint for Progress

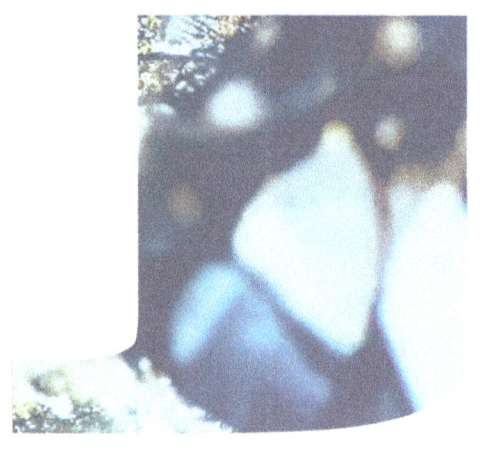

Monthly Inventory

books read:

1
2
3
4
5

new learning/new experience/new connection:

risks taken:

accomplishments or favorite happenings:

contributions to the world:

DAILY CHECKLIST

	M	T	W	Th	F	Sa	Su
Did I initiate conversation with a stranger?							
Did I initiate conversation with a stranger? Did I offer assistance, deep listening or a compliment to someone?							
Did I initiate conversation with a stranger? *Did I offer assistance, deep listening or a compliment to someone?* Did I offer a contribution or gesture anonymously?							
Did I initiate conversation with a stranger? *Did I offer assistance, deep listening or a compliment to someone?* *Did I offer a contribution or gesture anonymously?* Did I do something I didn't want to do that is good for me (like pushups)?							

#SHINE

abandoned, absent-minded, accepted, affectionate, afraid, aggravated, aggressive, agreeable, alienated, amazed, amused, angry, annoyed, anxious, apathetic, ashamed, astonished, arrogant, aversion, avoidance, awed, baffled, bashful, bewildered, bitter, bored, bothered, brave, brilliant, calm, caring, cautious, clever, cheerful, compassionate, competent, concealment, confident, confused, considerate, content, cooperative, courageous, craving, critical, curious, daring, deceitful, defiant, delighted, depressed, despair, destructive, detached, determined, devious, devastate, diligence, disappointed, disapproving, discouraged, disillusioned, dismayed, disorganized, disrespectful, distant, distracted, doubt, eager, ecstatic, embarrassed, empathetic, empty, energetic, encouraged, enraged, excited, enthusiastic, envious, equanimity, excited, exhausted, exuberant, fearful, flustered, foolish, forgetful, forgiving, fortunate, free, friendly, frightened, frustrated, fulfilled, furious, generous, grateful, greedy, grief-stricken, guilty, happy, hateful, heartbroken, helpless, hesitant, hopeful, hopeless, honest, honored, hostile, humble, humiliated, hurt, ignorant, ignored, impatient, important, inadequate, indifferent, inferior, infuriated, inquisitive, insecure, insignificant, inspired, interested, intimate, invisible, irrational, irresponsible, irritated, isolated, jealous, joyful, judgmental, kind, lack of faith, lazy, leery, liberated, light-hearted, likable, loathing, lonely, loving, lonely, lost, lucky, mad, magical, malicious, manipulated, manipulative, maternal, mean, meek, melodramatic, mischievous, miserable, mistrustful, misunderstood, mixed-up, moody, naive, needed, needy, neglected, neglectful, nervous, nice, noisy, nonchalant, obedient, obligated, obsessive, obstinate, offended, open, optimistic, out-of-control, outraged, overjoyed, overloaded, overstimulated, overwhelmed, panicked, patronized, peaceful, pensive, perplexed, petulant, petty, playful, pleased, powerful, powerless, preoccupied, proud, puzzled, qualified, quarrelsome, quiet, quirky, rageful, rational, rattled, reactive, ready, reasonable, reassured, rebellious, refreshed, rejected, relaxed, relieved, reluctant, remorseful, resentful, reserved, respected, rested, restless, sad, safe, sarcastic, satisfied, scared, scornful, secure, sensitive, serene, serious, shocked, shy, skeptical, startled, submissive, surprised, suspicious, smiley, smug, sociable, sorry, spiteful, stable, stressed, stubborn, suspicious, talkative, tearful, temperamental, terrified, thankful, thoughtful, threatened, timid, tired, touched, torn, troubled, trusted, trustworthy, ugly, unappreciated, uncertain, uncomfortable, undecided, understood, understanding, uneasy, unimpressed, unique, useless, valued, vain, vibrant, victimized, victorious, violent, vital, vivacious, volatile, vulnerable, warm, weak, weary, weepy, well, whimsical, willful, wishful, wistful, withdrawn, witty, woeful, worthless, worried, worthless, wronged, yearning, yielding, youthful

August

Describe your deepest feelings.

August

Monthly Inventory

books read:

1
2
3
4
5

new learning/new experience/new connection:

risks taken:

accomplishments or favorite happenings:

contributions to the world:

DAILY CHECKLIST

	M	T	W	Th	F	Sa	Su
Did I do what I wanted as opposed to "what I had to do"?							
Did I recognize stress and adjust my actions or activities?							
Did I do what I wanted as opposed to "what I had to do"?							
Did I recognize stress and adjust my actions or activities?							

#SHINE

September

Notes to remember about past three goals:

What did I do well?

How can I improve and advance?

Write 3 more goals for the next 3 months.

1._____

Why is this goal important?
What ACTION will you add to achieve this goal?
When?

2._____

Why is this goal important?
What ACTION will you add to achieve this goal?
When?

3._____

Why is this goal important?
What ACTION will you add to achieve this goal?
When?

Add ACTIONS to calendar dates!

Monthly Inventory

books read:

1
2
3
4
5

new learning/new experience/new connection:

risks taken:

accomplishments or favorite happenings:

contributions to the world:

DAILY CHECKLIST

	M	T	W	Th	F	Sa	Su
Did I offer service to others?							
Did I act kind when not feeling kind?							
Did I use words love/like/fond and use less self-references me/myself/I?							
Did I abstain from taking things personally?							

#SHINE

October

Describe your best possible self.

Monthly Inventory

books read:

1
2
3
4
5

new learning/new experience/new connection:

risks taken:

accomplishments or favorite happenings:

contributions to the world:

DAILY CHECKLIST

	M	T	W	Th	F	Sa	Su
Did I practice mindfulness/meditation?							
Did I practice reflection/self-inventory?							
Did I practice getting outside of myself?							
Did I practice owning mistakes?							

#SHINE

November

What have I done well this year?

What can I do differently in the future?

Nove

Monthly Inventory

books read:

1
2
3
4
5

new learning/new experience/new connection:

risks taken:

accomplishments or favorite happenings:

contributions to the world:

DAILY CHECKLIST

	M	T	W	Th	F	Sa	Su
Did I contribute to my purpose and/or feel fulfilled in some way?							
Did I contribute to my purpose and/or feel fulfilled in some way?							
Did I contribute to my purpose and/or feel fulfilled in some way?							
Did I contribute to my purpose and/or feel fulfilled in some way?							

#SHINE

December

What is great about my life today?

mber

Monthly Inventory

books read:

1
2
3
4
5

new learning/new experience/new connection:

risks taken:

accomplishments or favorite happenings:

contributions to the world:

DAILY CHECKLIST

	M	T	W	Th	F	Sa	Su
Did I leave the world a little better?							
Did I leave the world a little better?							
Did I leave the world a little better?							
Did I leave the world a little better?							

#SHINE

Activities

Jan	Feb	Mar	Apr	May	JunE

Calendar

July	Aug	Sept	Oct	Nov	Dec

"One of the most important writing techniques for boosting happiness revolves around the psychology of gratitude...those expressing gratitude ended up happier, much more optimistic about the future, and physically healthier--and they even exercised more." -Richard Wiseman

GRATITUDE ALPHABET (something to be grateful for using each letter)

A

B

C

D

E

F

G

H

I

J

K

L

M

N

O

P

Q

R

S

T

U

V

W

X

Y

Z

www.ingramcontent.com/pod-product-compliance
Lightning Source LLC
Chambersburg PA
CBHW061151010526
44118CB00026B/2941